END

Ready for lift-off?
Log your name here

....

Dedicated to Dexter, Wilfred and Sadie.
- BN

Professor Astro Cat's Solar System © Flying Eye Books 2017.

This is a first edition published in 2017 by Flying Eye Books,
an imprint of Nobrow Ltd. 27 Westgate Street, London E8 3RL.

Illustrations by Ben Newman. Text by Dr Dominic Walliman and Hanna Milner.
Dominic Walliman and Ben Newman have asserted their right
under the Copyright, Designs and Patents Act, 1988,
to be identified as the Author and Illustrator of this Work.

Published in the US by Nobrow (US) Inc.
Printed in Poland on FSC® certified paper.

ISBN: 978-1-911171-37-9

Order from www.flyingeyebooks.com

PROFESSOR ASTRO CAT'S
SOLAR SYSTEM

DR DOMINIC WALLIMAN & BEN NEWMAN

·FLYING EYE BOOKS·

LONDON | NEW YORK

WELCOME TO OUR SOLAR SYSTEM

Hello, planet explorers! We're about to set off on a tour of our solar system.

Look at that view!

MARS

EARTH

MERCURY

VENUS

THE SUN

The solar system first began as a giant cloud of dust and gas. It slowly joined together to make the Sun and the eight **planets**.

NEPTUNE

ASTEROID BELT

SATURN

JUPITER

URANUS

The planets all move in circles called **orbits** around the Sun. It is a star and our first stop.

Off we go!

THE SUN

Sunglasses on, everyone! Remember not to look directly at the Sun. The light is so bright that it could damage your eyes.

We see the Sun travel across the sky every day, but it is not really moving. It is actually the Earth that is spinning round and round.

The Sun is a giant fireball. It gives light and heat to all living things on Earth. Whew, it's too hot here! Next stop, Mercury.

MERCURY

Mercury is the closest planet to the Sun and the smallest planet in our solar system.

It has no **atmosphere**. This means that it is not protected against asteroids and comets. Its surface is covered in holes!

MESSENGER

We learned a lot about Mercury from a **space probe** called Messenger. It showed that there is ice on Mercury. Pretty cool, huh?

Ah, this is my favourite planet of all... Earth! It is the perfect distance from the Sun for liquid water to exist. All plants and animals need water to live.

When one side of Earth faces the Sun, we call this daytime. The side facing away experiences night time. A full day and night lasts 24 hours, as that is how long it takes Earth to spin around once.

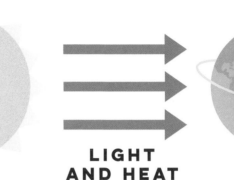

SUN

LIGHT
AND HEAT

EARTH

THE MOON

The **moon** is our closest neighbour in space! It takes about a month to **orbit** around Earth.

MARS

Seeing red? We must be on Mars!
Mars is a very dry planet, like a desert. Its red colour comes from the rocks on its surface.

There are marks on the surface of Mars that show where water flows. This has made scientists wonder if there used to be life on Mars.

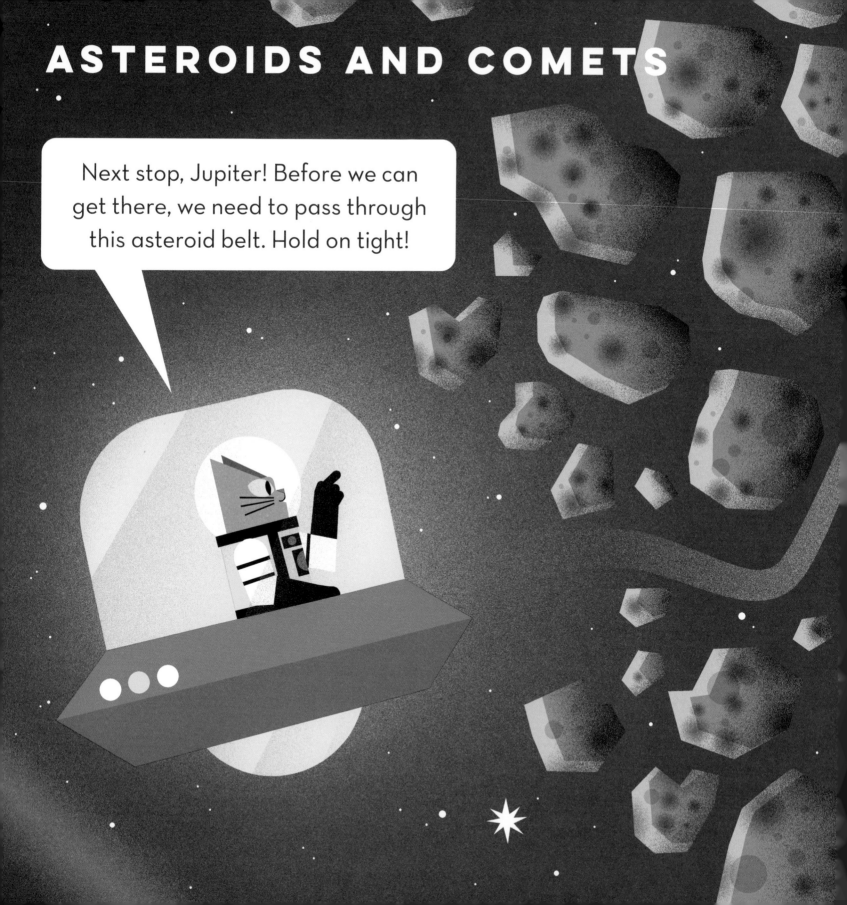

JUPITER

Whew! We made it. The last four planets in our solar system are mostly made of gases. We can't land on their surface, as we would fall straight through.

Quite right. But this planet is so big, it's better to see it from a distance. Here is the giant Jupiter.

There are over sixty **moons orbiting** Jupiter. One of them, Europa, is the most likely place in the solar system to have **extraterrestrial life**.

SATURN

What a jewel! All of the gas planets have rings, but Saturn's are the biggest in the solar system. They are made of tiny chunks of ice.

Saturn is the furthest planet from Earth that can be easily seen without a telescope.

Guess what? Even though Saturn is really big, it could float on water!

URANUS

Uranus is the only planet in our solar system that spins on its side! Something huge must have crashed into it, billions of years ago.

NEPTUNE

Neptune is named after the Roman god of the sea because of its beautiful blue colour.

The wind on the surface of this planet is the fastest in the whole solar system!

OBSERVING THE SOLAR SYSTEM AND BEYOND

What a trip! Now that we're on Earth, let's study the planets and the stars. Almost everything we know about space has been discovered through telescopes. They help us see things that are very far away.

GLOSSARY

Atmosphere The blanket of gases around a planet.

Extraterrestrial life The proper term for aliens, which are living things that exist somewhere other than Earth. Scientists have not found any real evidence of them yet.

Moon An object that orbits around a planet.

Orbit The oval-shaped movement of a planet or moon around a star or another planet.

Planet A large mass of rock or gas that orbits a star.

Space Probe A spacecraft for exploring space and other planets. It is controlled by computers back on Earth.